My Totally Awesome

Travel Fun Book

An Activity Book & Travel Diary

© 2001 Specialty Book Marketing, Inc., New York, NY 10016

ISBN 1-882663-52-7

Published by:
Plymouth Press, Ltd.
101 Panton Road
Vergennes, VT 05491
On the Web: www.plymouthpress.com

First edition production by Brad Reed Design Works

Cover art by Darin Maloney

Plymouth Press has extensive experience in formulating special editions of our books for educational or promotional purposes. Regular and special editions of this book are available at a significant discount when purchaed in bulk quantities. To discuss options or for a free quote, call our marketing manager at 800.350.1007.

Printed in the USA

PLANNING MAKES A BIG DIFFERENCE!

CHAPTER 1

VACATION PLANS

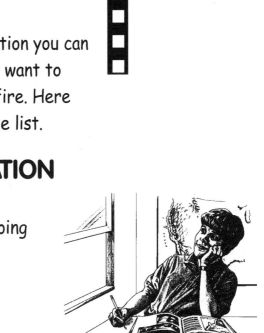

When you first find out that you'll be going on vacation, you can picture in your mind all of the things you have to look forward to and all the fun you will have. A vacation is an adventure and you want it to be great! If you plan ahead, you will enjoy doing all the things you have planned. Believe it or not, you'll enjoy the surprises even more.

If you know what you want from this vacation you can plan how to achieve it. For example, you might want to learn how to surf, milk a cow, or make a campfire. Here are some all-purpose aims. Add your own to the list.

WHAT I WANT TO DO ON VACATION

1- Have the most fun I can
2- Learn about people and the place I'm going
3- Get a souvenir to keep
4- Have good memories

WHAT ELSE?

5- _____
6- _____
7- _____
8- _____

THE PLACE WE'RE GOING

Try to learn about the place you are going so you can plan how you want to spend your time. Is it a famous or historic place? Did any well-known people live or work there? Did something special happen there to make the place important?

You may visit more than one place. List them.

Country _____ **State** _____ **City** _____

THE NAME GAME

What does the name of the place you are going mean? How did it get its name? There is an interesting story behind every name.

Here are the names of some of the states in America and the stories behind them. If you want to find out the meaning and the story behind the name of the place you are going, do what baseball manager Casey Stengel suggested, "You could look it up!" You can also have some fun trying to guess or make up some stories.

CONNECTICUT is from an Indian word "quinnehtukqut" (sound it out). It means "next to the long river."

GEORGIA is named after King George II of England.

INDIANA means "land of Indians."

LOUISIANA means "land of Louis" and was named for King Louis XIV of France.

MARYLAND is named for a woman (surprise!) Henrietta Maria, the queen of Charles I of England. (They might have called it Henriettaland!)

MASSACHUSETTS is from two Indian words meaning "great mountain place."

DELAWARE was named from the Delaware River, which was named for Lord De La Warr, who was a Governor of Virginia.

NEVADA is a Spanish word meaning "snow-capped," describing mountains there.

VERMONT comes from two French words: "vert" (green) and "mont" (mountain).

THE NICKNAME GAME

Nicknames are fun, unless they're unkind. We're talking *good* here, like Darryl "Strawman" Strawberry. You get a nickname because of something about you. If a girl is called "Blondie" it's because she has blonde hair.

Places have nicknames too. Here are some states and their nicknames. Try to figure out how they got them.

1- **WASHINGTON** is called **THE EVERGREEN STATE**

2- **OKLAHOMA** is called **THE SOONER STATE**

3- **UTAH** is called **THE BEEHIVE STATE**

4- **NEW HAMPSHIRE** is called **THE GRANITE STATE**

5- **TENNESSEE** is called **THE VOLUNTEER STATE**

6- **OREGON** is called **THE BEAVER STATE**

7- **COLORADO** is called **THE CENTENNIAL STATE**

Here's why...

1- The state is covered with fir trees that are green all year.

2- Pioneer settlers tried to get land grants by sneaking into the territory <u>sooner</u> than they should in order to beat others to the land.

3- Utah's state symbols are a bee and hive because the people admire bees' industriousness.

4- The state has many stone quarries to mine granite for building.

5- A large number of men from Tennessee volunteered in the war against Mexico (Remember the Alamo!)

6- Many clever, eager beavers live in Oregon.

7- Colorado was admitted to the Union on the 100th anniversary of the signing of the Declaration of Independence.

Perhaps you can make up a nickname for the area you're going to. Be sure there's a good reason for your choice.

FREE INFORMATION IF YOU ASK

Many places have helpful guidebooks written about them. But if you have a tight budget you can get free information about many vacation spots. Ask for books from the library that will tell you about the place you are going. You can get maps and materials from auto clubs and travel agents, too.

Chapter 7 of this book has a list of Tourist Information offices in the United States, Canada and Mexico. Find the one nearest the place you are going and call or write to them for any information they will send you for free.

• Try to call or write for free information five or six weeks before you leave so the material will arrive in time to help you plan your trip!

Some special things to do and see at the place(s) we are going:

1. _____

2. _____

3. _____

4. _____

5. _____

GETTING THERE

In the frame below, draw or cut and paste a picture of the type of transportation you will use to travel. It could be a car, bus, train, plane, boat, or maybe an RV. It could be more than one kind of transportation.

TRAVEL DATA:

We will travel by _____

We are going to _____

It should take _____ to get there.

ABOUT TIME TRAVEL

The forty-eight states (not counting Alaska and Hawaii) and the Canadian Provinces are divided into FOUR time zones. There is a map in the front of your telephone directory which shows where the time zone dividing lines are. The time in the zone you are in is one hour later than the zone directly to the west of it and one hour earlier than the zone directly to the east of it.

If you are having lunch at noon in Chicago, Illinois, it is already 1:00 PM in New York, and it is only 11:00 AM in Denver. And your friends in California aren't even thinking about lunch because it's only 10:00 AM there! Use the time zone map to help you figure out how the time zones work.

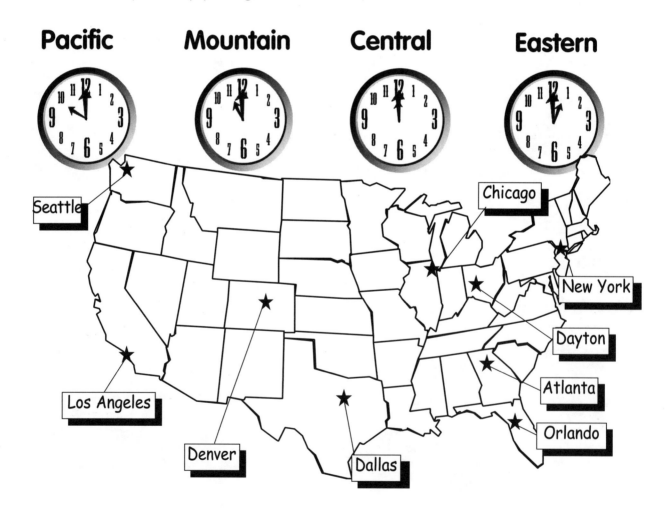

VACATION PLANS

HELP TOM UNDERSTAND TIME TRAVEL

Tom just looked at his tickets for his trip to California and he's worried. Tom will get on a plane at 9:00 AM in Dayton, Ohio, for a 35 minute flight to Chicago. In Chicago his travel agent has booked him on a flight to Los Angles that also leaves at 9:00 AM! And that's not all that Tom is worried about. His flight to Los Angeles is 3 hours long, and his friend said he would meet him at the airport at 10:00 AM! Can you explain to Tom how he'll be at the Los Angeles airport at 10:00 AM?

Think about it... Tom is leaving home at 9:00 AM and is traveling for 3 hours and 35 minutes. But when he lands at his destination, it will be 10:00 AM!

Will you cross time zones and be a time traveler? If you will, figure out how much time you will gain or lose when you travel across time zones.

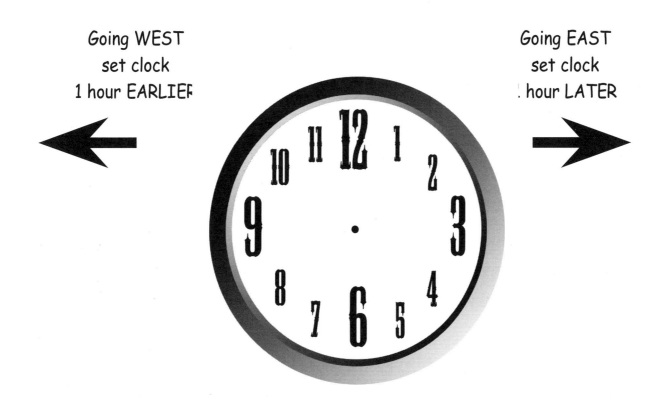

Going WEST
set clock
1 hour EARLIER

Going EAST
set clock
1 hour LATER

KEEPING EVERYONE HAPPY

You can be the star of this road show by keeping everyone in good spirits. You can be so great at this that no one will ever want to go anyplace without you. The secret is simple. Think of the things or activities that entertain each person on the list and make a list of those things.
For example:

NAME	HAPPY ACTIVITIES
Mom	singing
Dad	word games
Brother	jokes and riddles
Sister	eating snacks
Friend	making faces

Make your list for your fellow travellers. Add a deck of cards, colored pencils and a sharpener, dice ...and don't forget the snacks.

 # WHO'S GOING

NAME	HAPPY ACTIVITIES	THINGS TO BRING
_____	_____	_____
_____	_____	_____
_____	_____	_____
_____	_____	_____
_____	_____	_____
_____	_____	_____
_____	_____	_____

MY TRAVEL CALENDAR

Fill in the calendar below to make your travel calendar. Put in the name of the month and the dates.

MONTH _____ YEAR _____

	DATE	DATE
SUNDAY		
MONDAY		
TUESDAY		
WEDNESDAY		
THURSDAY		
FRIDAY		
SATURDAY		

- Put a star (★) in the day you will begin your trip.
- Color the travel days in with yellow or another light color.
- Pencil in any stops you'll make or special events already planned.

Don't forget to write:

- Put your friends' names on the days you want to send them postcards or letters. Send cards early so they are delivered before you get home. Don't forget Grandma and Grandpa! You know they are thinking about you.

DAY-BY-DAY PLANNER

Now that you have a general plan, you can make a day-by-day schedule so you'll have the most fun. Try to fit in all of the things you want to do, but make sure you don't try to do too much!

Remember, this is just your plan, and things will come up that you aren't aware of the first time you go to a place.

Don't forget you need time to rest, and it is important to eat well. If you miss a meal, have a healthy snack that's easy to carry and eat on the move. Some examples are raisins or an apple.

Be sure to leave a few moments each day to keep your vacation diary!

DAY 1   **Today's Date** _____

Special activities planned for today: _____

_____

Breakfast _____

Morning _____

_____

Lunch _____

Afternoon_____

_____

Dinner _____

Evening _____

_____

VACATION PLANS

DAY 2   **Today's Date** _____

Special activities planned for today: _____

_____

Breakfast _____

Morning _____

_____

Lunch _____

Afternoon _____

_____

Dinner _____

Evening _____

_____

DAY 3   **Today's Date** _____

Special activities planned for today: _____

_____

Breakfast _____

Morning _____

_____

Lunch _____

Afternoon _____

_____

Dinner _____

Evening _____

_____

VACATION PLANS

DAY 4   **Today's Date** _____

Special activities planned for today: _____
_____

Breakfast _____
Morning _____
_____

Lunch _____
Afternoon _____
_____

Dinner _____
Evening _____
_____

DAY 5   **Today's Date** _____

Special activities planned for today: _____
_____

Breakfast _____
Morning _____
_____

Lunch _____
Afternoon _____
_____

Dinner _____
Evening _____
_____

VACATION PLANS

DAY 6   **Today's Date** _____

Special activities planned for today: _____

_____

Breakfast _____

Morning _____

_____

Lunch _____

Afternoon_____

_____

Dinner _____

Evening _____

_____

DAY 7   **Today's Date** _____

Special activities planned for today: _____

_____

Breakfast _____

Morning _____

_____

Lunch _____

Afternoon_____

_____

Dinner _____

Evening _____

_____

C H A P T E R

2

READY...SET...GO!

GET READY: FOUR SPECIAL PACKING LISTS OF MY THINGS

Packing is a very important step in having an enjoyable vacation. You should have all you need, but not so much that it's hard to travel. You need to take some things no matter where you go. Other things depend on **where** you're going, **what** you'll be doing, and what the **weather** will be like. Here are some checklists to help you pack. Think of all the stuff you'll need and put it on the lists. It's important to think of everything, but you can't take everything! Remember, you're going on vacation, not moving!

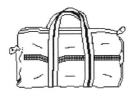

1- THINGS I NEED EVERYWHERE

North or South or East or West
In sunshine, rain, or snow
I have special things I need to take
No matter where I go.

identification card

toothbrush & paste

belt pack/backpack, wallet

comb & brush

stamps

spending money

phone #'s & addresses

emergency money

camera, film & flashbulbs

pen, pencil & paper

batteries

2- SPECIAL THINGS I WILL NEED ON <u>THIS</u> TRIP

It will be Winter Summer Spring Fall where I'm going

It will be Cold Hot Fair when I am there

This list is right for the time and place

Now I'll pack it all with care.

Circle one of the four seasons.

Circle the right weather word.

3- THINGS FOR REST AND RELAXATION

I'll take this book and a game I like

And maybe a deck of cards

So no matter what the weather is

I'll have fun against all odds.

a pair of dice for games

4- THINGS THAT JUST DON'T FIT

It seems as though I packed too much.
I must leave some things behind.
It will all be here when I return,
So really I don't mind.

_____   _____

_____   _____

_____   _____

_____   _____

THINGS FOR EVERYONE

Your folks will pack all the important papers and things you'll need for your trip. A medical kit for headaches, tummy aches, and scrapes is very important. You must take identification for each traveller, emergency telephone numbers, and any special needs of each person. Know what important things have been packed and list them.

There are some things we have to take
Anywhere where we go
Like medicine and first aid stuff
Everyone should know

_____   _____

_____   _____

_____   _____

CHAPTER 3

ON THE WAY

ON THE WAY

Safety and Comfort

Remember this simple rhyme to keep your vacation fun

Think of your health and safety first
Avoid what could make this trip your worst!

Hints & Tips for a Healthy Trip

1- Be careful what you eat. Check with your folks if there are foods you should not have.

2- Try not to miss meals. Carry a healthy snack like raisins, an apple or other fruit.

3- Be sure you get enough sleep.

4- In a plane chew gum or suck on a hard candy during take offs and landings so your ears don't pop!

5- Know where your family keeps the first aid kit.

6- On long trips, stand and stretch every couple of hours. The driver should stop to let you do this so you don't get restless.

Hints & Tips for a Safe Trip

1- Always use a safety belt in a plane or car.

2- In a plane read the safety instruction card and listen carefully to the instructions of the crew.

3- Stay with your group and don't go wandering off on your own.

4- Each day carry the name, address and phone number of where you are staying.

Here are some tips if you get lost:

1- Always have coins for the telephone.

2- Try to contact the adults you are travelling with immediately.

3- Only ask for help from a policeman or policewoman.

4- If you can't find a policeman, use a pay phone and call your hotel. Tell them the two streets nearest the phone and if there is a number on the phone tell them that too. If you have a problem with this, call 911 or the operator and ask for the police.

DO NOT ASK A STRANGER, and <u>never go with a stranger or get into a stranger's car!</u>

Have a plan. Ask the adults you're travelling with what you should do if you get lost or separated from the group. Know what they want you to do if you do get lost, and keep calm and do it. That will help them find you.

Fill in this little card, cut it out, and carry it with you on your trip.

You can write your emergency plan or any special information on the back of this card. Keep it with you in case of emergency, but the best thing you can do is to **stay alert** and **pay attention**.

My home phone number is

(　　) _____

Emergency phone number

(　　) _____

Ask to speak to

_____

I need help!

My name is

_____

I am staying at _____

_____

Phone number _____

Travel Manners

ON THE ROAD

Whether you're in your own car or on a plane, train, or bus with many other people, you have to be considerate of your fellow travellers so everyone will have a good time. If you have a radio, use earphones. On long trips everyone gets tired of sitting in one place, not just you. Instead of running around, play the travel games in this book. Travelling is much more fun if you are considerate of others.

A GUEST IS NOT A PEST

Whether you're staying in one place or making many stops, be sure your manners check in with you. At hotels and motels, other guests may have come for different reasons than you did. President Washington often went places just to sleep. You'll have even more fun if you're not in trouble for splashing in the pool, turning the TV too loud, or banging on the soda machine

If you need to be wild, ask if you can vacation in the great outdoors. But be careful, if you upset bears or other wild animals, they can be more dangerous than angry hotel managers!

If I get lost I should . . .

_____

_____

_____

_____

LET'S EAT

If you are on a camping trip, you really are eating out! Remember to clean up carefully so uninvited animals don't come in the night to finish your meal.

If you're not on a camping trip, you'll probably get the chance to eat in a nice restaurant. This is a treat that you may never have again if you don't bring your good manners to the table. If you can correctly answer the five questions below, you can eat in any restaurant and you will be welcome back anytime.

1- When the waiter says, "Hello, my name is Bruce. I'll be your waiter tonight," you should —

    a) Say, "Yo, Dude, I'm _____ and boy am I hungry!"

    b) Say, "Hey Bruce, how are the wife and kids?"

    c) Smile and say, "Hello."

2-There are no pizzas, hamburgers, or hot dogs on the menu. You should —

    a) Demand to leave right away.

    b) Complain and refuse to eat anything.

    c) Ask the waiter or others at the table for a suggestion.

3- You decide to try an olive and the one you're eating has a pit in it. You

    a) Swallow it.

    b) Spit it out under the table.

    c) Take it out of your mouth with your fingers and put it on your plate.

4- You accidently knock over your giant root beer float. You should

    a) Hold up the empty glass and yell, "Yo Bruce, another one of these!"

    b) Laugh and yell, "Man the lifeboats."

    c) Mop up what you can with your napkin until Bruce comes to take care of it.

5- Your favorite song is played on the background music. You should

    a) Sing along to entertain everyone while they eat.

    b) Drum along with your silverware or get up and dance.

    c) Remark how good the song is and enjoy listening to it.

DID YOU NOTICE ALL THE CORRECT ANSWERS ARE "C" ? You can write about the restaurants and your favorite meals in your travel diary. If you ever go to the same place again, you'll know where you can get food you like.

TRAVEL GAMES YOU CAN PLAY ANYWHERE

CHAPTER 4

GAMES FOR THE ROAD

You probably packed a deck of cards, dice, and if you own it, a hand held electronic game. If the batteries go dead, or it makes too much noise, you can play any of these games for fun on the way or in your room (or tent). For some games you don't need anything but your smarts. For others, you need a pencil and paper or dice. First read the instructions carefully and the games will be easy.

1- I SPY...

This is a fun game to play if you are travelling through nice scenery. Looking out the window is fun, and you see many things you don't see at home. This is how to play:

One player is the "SPY." Everyone looks around and the Spy picks something and says "I spy something and it begins with the letter ___" and he says the letter. Everyone else tries to guess what the object is. The person who guesses correctly is the next to be the Spy. Be fair, and don't pick something that goes by too quickly. You may choose something inside the car, train, or plane. If an object outside the vehicle is selected, once it is out of sight, another must be chosen, unless you are going through a forest and you picked a tree.

2- BACKPACK

The first player starts by choosing an item to finish the sentence: "In my backpack I put a _____." He may say "<u>comb</u>."

The next player repeats what the first person packed and adds something else: "In my backpack I put a comb and a <u>sweater</u>."

Everybody repeats and adds. Finally you may have this kind of sentence: "In my backpack I put a comb, a sweater, a deck of cards, a T-shirt, etc."

Anyone who leaves an item out or maybe mixes up the order (that's up to you) is out. The one remembering to pack all the items in the correct order wins.

3- I AM VERY FAMOUS !

This guessing game is easy to play, but you must play fairly. One person thinks of a famous person from real life or from a story. He starts the game

by saying, "I'm very famous." This is the signal for the others to begin taking turns asking questions to guess who the famous person is. Ask very general questions at the start to narrow down the choices. "Are you a real person?" is a good question, since someone could pick a cartoon character. And the famous person cannot lie! If you were to pick <u>Michelangelo</u> as your famous person, you could not switch back and forth between the Italian painter and sculptor from the 1500's and the 20th century

Ninja Turtle with the same name. The player who guesses the famous person correctly becomes the next famous person. If nobody guesses correctly, then the player must say who he is and gets another turn. However, if the other players think his choice was too difficult, they can agree that another player takes a turn.

4- <u>WHAT'S A WIDGET ???</u>

This game can get very funny. One player is chosen to start the game. He thinks of an ordinary object and begins the game by saying, "I've got a widget." The other players take turns asking questions to try to figure out what the 'widget' really is. The questions should be about anything. The owner of the widget must include the secret object in each answer, calling it a widget and making the answer a clue. For example, suppose the object is a baseball bat, and the first question is , "Have you read any good books lately?" The widget owner can answer, "No, I've been playing with my widget." To the question "Will it rain tomorrow?" the owner can say, "If it does I can't play with my widget." This is a hard game, but if you play honestly, you'll laugh a lot.

5- <u>WHO'S IN THERE?</u>

Can you find the name of a person in the list of car names? For example, if you mix up the letters in the word LINCOLN, you'll find the name COLIN. And lucky ROSE is in a PORSCHE. There may even be more than one person in a car. Find the people listed on the right in the cars listed on the left. In fact, there is A COP in one and you can find interesting things such as the word TOOT in one of the cars. Match the car numbers to

CARS		NAMES	
1	LINCOLN	A	ROSE
2	CHEVROLET	B	BUCK
3	PLYMOUTH	C	LEO (he's in 2 car:
4	FORD	D	TOTO
5	PONTIAC	E	ANN
6	TOYOTA	F	ROD
7	CADILLAC	G	NAT
8	MITSUBISHI	H	TOM
9	NISSAN	I	CHER
10	BUICK	J	CAL
11	OLDSMOBILE	K	TIM
12	PORSCHE	L	COLIN

the letter of the name you find in the car. You may find more people in the cars than we did! Don't peek at the answers below until you're done.

ANSWERS: 1-L, 2-I, 3-H, 4-F, 5-G, 6-D, 7-J, 8-K, 9-E, 10-B, 11-C, 12-A. A COP is in Pontiac and TOOT is in Toyota.

Who else can you find?

6-ALPHABET TRAVEL

You give your imagination and memory a workout with this game. Decide who will go first. Beginning with the letter <u>A</u> name a place to go and a thing to find there that both begin with <u>A</u>. The next person repeats these things and adds a <u>B</u> place and thing. It will go like this: The first person says, "We're going to <u>A</u>lbany to get <u>A</u>pples." The second person says, "We're going to <u>A</u>lbany to get <u>A</u>pples and to <u>B</u>oston to get <u>B</u>eans." The third person then repeats these and adds a <u>C</u> place and thing. If you're competitive, each mistake disqualifies a player. If you're playing for memory fun, you can help each other out. It might help to skip real hard letters like <u>Q</u> or <u>X</u>.

7 - FOLLOW THE LETTER

Compared with Alphabet Travel, this game is easy! Everyone goes to a destination that begins with the last letter of the previous player's place. For example, Player One starts by saying, "We're going to Tennesse<u>e</u>." The next player must pick a place that begins with <u>E</u>, and might say, "Then we'll go to Egyp<u>t</u>." The next player must take everyone to a <u>T</u> place. "Then we're going to Timbukt<u>u</u>," "Then we're going to Uta<u>h</u>" and so on until you've gone as many places as you can without repeating one. You can play using only cities, countries or states, or using every place in the world.

ABCDEFGHIJKLMNOPQRSTUVWXYZ

8 - WHAT'S IN A NAME?

You'll really have to think to be good at this game! Once you have the hang of it, you'll have lots of fun. Begin by using your first name. For each letter of your name, you must choose a word that describes you. For example, this is what Willy, Delia, and Casey thought of:

W	Wise	D	Dainty	C	Clever
I	Intelligent	E	Entertaining	A	Active
L	Likeable	L	Lively	S	Sweet
L	Lean	I	Interesting	E	Energetic
Y	Young	A	Alive	Y	Yankee

If you want to make it a little more interesting, you can try to make the words form a sentence, as John and Fran did.

J	Jump	F	Find
O	On	R	Right
H	Hard	A	Answers
N	Nuts	N	Now

Play this game with your name. Try to think of a sentence that has something to do with your trip.

9 - CONVERTIBLES

This game can be played with pencil and paper, each player making a list. It can also be played orally with everybody taking turns changing one letter of the previous player's word. You chain until you can go no further.

This is how the written version is played:

Everybody starts with the same 3-letter word. Make a new word by changing one letter and keeping two. Try to make 5 new words, then compare lists. You get one point for each word no one else has on his list. For instance:

Start with any 3-letter word and go on as long as possible. After you're an expert at this, try a harder version, "Changing Words."

10 - CHANGING WORDS

This game will make you wonder how many words you know. There are pairs of words listed below. You start with one word, and by changing one letter at a time, you change it into the other word. Each time you change a letter, you must still have a real word. The fewest words you need to get to the finish, the better. For example, it is easy to change **BOY** to **MAN** like this:

BOY changes to **BAY**, then to **MAY**, then to **MAN**

Try changing these words from the one on the left to the one on the right:

POP into **MOM**	**DOG** into **CAT**
BAY into **SEA**	**POT** into **PAN**
MOO into **BAA**	**GIVE** into **TAKE**
SICK into **WELL**	**LOOK** into **WINK**
CAR into **BUS**	**FAST** into **SLOW**

Here are some possible solutions:

POP	MOP					MOM
BAY	BAT	SAT	SET			SEA
MOO	BOO	BOA				BAA
SICK	SILK	SILL	SELL			WELL
CAR	BAR	BAN	BUN			BUS
DOG	COG	COT				CAT
POT	PAT					PAN
GIVE	GAVE	GATE	RATE	RAKE		TAKE
LOOK	LOCK	LICK	LINK			WINK
FAST	LAST	LOST	LOOT	BOOT	BLOT	SLOT	SLOW

11 - HANGMAN

This word game is not as gruesome as it sounds. Players take turns being the hangman. The hangman thinks of a word that has between six and twelve letters, and the other players will try to guess it. The only clue they get is the number of letters in the word. The hangman draws a dash for each letter in the word. If someone guesses a letter in the word, the hangman writes it in. If the letter is not in the word, the hangman draws one line of the gallows. Try to guess the word before the hangman finishes! It might go like this:

The hangman thinks of the word RADICAL, and he draws seven dashes so the players know the word has seven letters.

    — — — — — — —

If a player guesses the letter A, the hangman must write in the two A's on the correct dashes.

    — A — — — A —

But if a player guesses T, the hangman begins to draw the gallows. The diagrams below show how the hangman adds one line for each wrong guess.

Players can have more guesses if the hangman has to draw eyes, nose, ears, mouth, hands and feet.

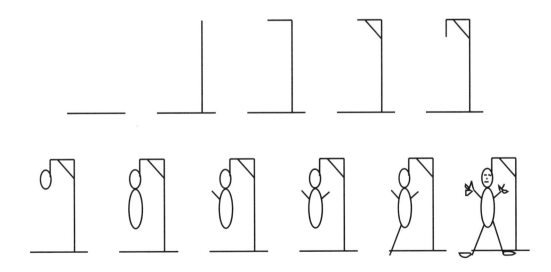

12 - COFFEEPOT

Everybody takes a turn being IT. The other players secretly choose a verb (an action word). IT tries to guess the mystery word by asking the other players questions using "coffeepot" for the secret word. The questions must be answered with a truthful "yes" or "no." For example, the secret action word might be "**run**" and IT begins by asking, "Do you **coffeepot** outside?" "Can you **coffeepot** in bed?" and so on. Each player gets a turn to be IT and the

player who guesses the secret word using the least number of questions is the winner.

13 - BUZZ BUZZ BUZZ BUZZ BUZZ BUZZ

First choose the order in which the players will take turns. Begin counting to 100, each player saying the next number when it is his turn. The trick is that the player who is supposed to say 7 says "buzz" instead of 7. After that, each number divisible by 7 isn't said. Instead, the player must say "buzz." To make this really hard, but more fun, say "buzz" for 7, "buzz, buzz" for 14, "buzz, buzz, buzz" for 21, and so on. A mistake and you're disqualified, or you can just play for laughs (or buzzes).

14 - STORY WORDS

Each player writes a 3-letter word at the top of a page and passes the page to the player on his left. Each player tries to write a sentence using each letter in the word at the top of the page to start a word in the sentence. If the word is **HAT**, the sentence could be **H**ave **A**nother **T**reat. After the sentence, write a 4-letter word and pass the paper again. The next round use a 5-letter word, then 6, and so on. The last player stumped is the winner.

15 - STORY CHAINS

Choose the order in which the players will take turns. The first player starts telling a story, making it up as he or she goes along. After a few sentences but before a minute is up, that person stops and the next player continues the story his or her way. The story must keep developing until everyone has a chance. You can keep going around depending on how funny the story is. Begin the story with "Once Upon A Time," and who knows where it will end! If you have a small tape recorder it is fun to tape and replay your multi-authored masterpiece.

16 - BIG INDIAN

You play this game with a deck of cards. Each player takes one card from the deck <u>without looking at it.</u> When everyone is ready, hold your card up on top of your head like a feather in a headdress so you can see the other players' cards (feathers) but you can't see your own. The highest card will win a feather, and the other players will lose a feather, unless they drop out. <u>You can bluff in this game,</u> so if you see a player with a high card, try to convince them it is very low and if they drop out you could be left with the highest card. After each player decides to stay in or drop out, the player with the highest card gets a feather. If you drop out, you can't win or lose a feather. The first to get six feathers wins.

17 - ARITHMEDICE

Take out the dice you brought with you. Each player takes a turn tossing the dice. Add up the numbers for your toss and write down the total. After five turns, total your totals and the highest number wins. You can also play this game by multiplying the numbers on the dice in each turn to get very high numbers.

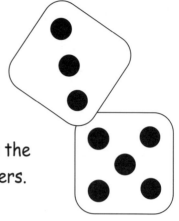

18 - GUGGENHEIM OR CATEGORIES

For this you need a pencil and paper. Draw a chart with six lines and six columns like the one below. In the top left hand box write your name. Pick five categories of items. They can be anything you like: sports figures, TV programs, fruits, names, animals, flowers, etc. Put your five topics in the first column under your name. Now choose any five letters of the alphabet and put one in each box in the top line next to your name.

When everyone is ready, begin to fill in the boxes with items that start with the letter at the top of the column and match the category at the left. If the category is Animals and the first letter is P, pony, porcupine, or pig would be right. Whoever has the most boxes filled in after 5 minutes is the winner.

Here's an example on one that Brad is working on.

BRAD	P	M	H	O	S
Animals	pony	moose		ox	
Flavors		maple			spearmint
Flowers	pansy		hyacinth	orchid	
Colors	purple				
names		Mary		Oliver	Sue

19 - THE PIRATE'S PARROT

"The Pirate's parrot is a(n)_____parrot and its name is _____."
Everybody in turn fills in the blanks with words that begin with "A"; as in "The Pirate's parrot is an <u>angry</u> parrot and its name is <u>Andy</u>." Then everybody tries it with all the other letters from B to Z. Some letters are very hard, so you can ask for help twice. Take turns being the first to go with each new letter.

20 -TRAVEL RIDDLES

Everybody loves to solve riddles. How good are you and your group at solving these travel riddles?

A- What's good about a ride in a taxi?
B- What driver is always turning but never gets a ticket?
C- When is a sailor not a sailor?
D- Beside paving it wider, how can you make a road broad?
E- FULL STOP. How do you spell it without any L's?
F- What land would little children and babies like to go to on vacation?
G- If you go to the beach why won't you get hungry?
H- What goes from north to south or east to west but never moves?

Answers:

A-The price is <u>fare</u>. **B**- A screwdriver. **C**-When he's aboard. **D**-Start it with a 'B'. **E**-
    IT. **F**-Lapland. **G**-Because of the sand which is there. **H**-A road.

21- SEE WHO CAN KEEP QUIET THE LONGEST

This game is usually suggested by the driver or some other travellers. Humor them and play it. After 10 minutes it is fair to end the game. It is also called **You Can Come Up For Air**. Pretend you are under water, but when you run out of breath you're allowed to take another. Don't hold your breath too long or you'll pass out!

CHAPTER 5

MY TRAVEL DIARY

A TRAVEL DIARY TO KEEP

A travel diary is fun to write and even more fun to have when the trip is over. Set aside some time each evening and write about all of the things you enjoyed during the day. Illustrate your diary with drawings, postcards, or photographs you have taken. If you like to take pictures and you take a lot, you might want to make a scrapbook of the photos and match them to your diary. When you get your pictures back, write the date and place each was taken under it so you'll always know exactly what the picture is and when you were there. If you like to draw, take a sketch pad and markers with you each day in your backpack. Match your sketches to your diary too.

Look back over your list of day plans. Write about all of the surprises that weren't part of the original plan. Things often happen to change your plans, especially when you go somewhere or do something for the first time.

Did you try new foods, make new friends, buy a souvenir or gift? Be sure to write the special things you'll want to tell your friends or relatives. Try not to forget anything! Use a page for each day, and if you need extra space, use loose paper. Put the date on the top of the paper and insert it in your diary where it belongs.

You can cut out and number the diary pages and put them into a notebook to keep as a permanent record of your vacation!

MY TRAVEL DIARY

Diary kept by

for the trip to

_____

in the year

_____

My Travel Diary

Today is [   ]   _The date is_ [   ]

A short list of TODAY'S special adventures

Someone I met: _____

Something special I saw: _____

Something new I learned: _____

Something I want to tell my friends about: _____

_____

Everything about TODAY: _____

_____

_____

_____

_____

_____

_____

_____

_____

_____

_____

_____

_____

My Travel Diary

PICTURE PAGE

On this page draw or paste pictures and photos of the things you saw.

My Travel Diary

Today is [_____]   *The date is* [_____]

A short list of TODAY'S special adventures

Someone I met: _____

Something special I saw: _____

Something new I learned: _____

Something I want to tell my friends about: _____
_____

Everything about TODAY: _____

_____

_____

_____

_____

_____

_____

_____

_____

_____

_____

_____

My Travel Diary

PICTURE PAGE

On this page draw or paste pictures and photos of the things you saw.

Page # _____

My Travel Diary

Today is | _____ | The date is | _____ |

A short list of TODAY'S special adventures

Someone I met: _____

Something special I saw: _____

Something new I learned: _____

Something I want to tell my friends about: _____
_____

Everything about TODAY: _____

_____

_____

_____

_____

_____

_____

_____

_____

_____

_____

_____

My Travel Diary

PICTURE PAGE

On this page draw or paste pictures and photos of the things you saw.

Page # _____

My Travel Diary

Today is [   ]   The date is [   ]

A short list of TODAY'S special adventures

Someone I met: _____

Something special I saw: _____

Something new I learned: _____

Something I want to tell my friends about: _____
_____

Everything about TODAY: _____

_____

_____

_____

_____

_____

_____

_____

_____

_____

_____

_____

My Travel Diary

PICTURE PAGE

On this page draw or paste pictures and photos of the things you saw.

Page # _____   **My Travel Diary**

Today is [   ]   The date is [   ]

A short list of TODAY'S special adventures

Someone I met: _____

Something special I saw: _____

Something new I learned: _____

Something I want to tell my friends about: _____

_____

Everything about TODAY: _____

_____

_____

_____

_____

_____

_____

_____

_____

_____

_____

_____

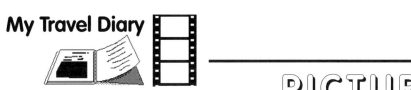

My Travel Diary

PICTURE PAGE

On this page draw or paste pictures and photos of the things you saw.

Page # _____

My Travel Diary

Today is [　　　　　] *The date is* [　　　　　]

A short list of TODAY'S special adventures

Someone I met: _____

Something special I saw: _____

Something new I learned: _____

Something I want to tell my friends about: _____

_____

Everything about TODAY: _____

_____

_____

_____

_____

_____

_____

_____

_____

_____

_____

_____

 **My Travel Diary**

PICTURE PAGE

On this page draw or paste pictures and photos of the things you saw.

Today is [   ] _The date is_ [   ]

A short list of TODAY'S special adventures

Someone I met: _____

Something special I saw: _____

Something new I learned: _____

Something I want to tell my friends about: _____
_____

Everything about TODAY: _____

_____

_____

_____

_____

_____

_____

_____

_____

_____

_____

My Travel Diary

PICTURE PAGE

On this page draw or paste pictures and photos of the things you saw.

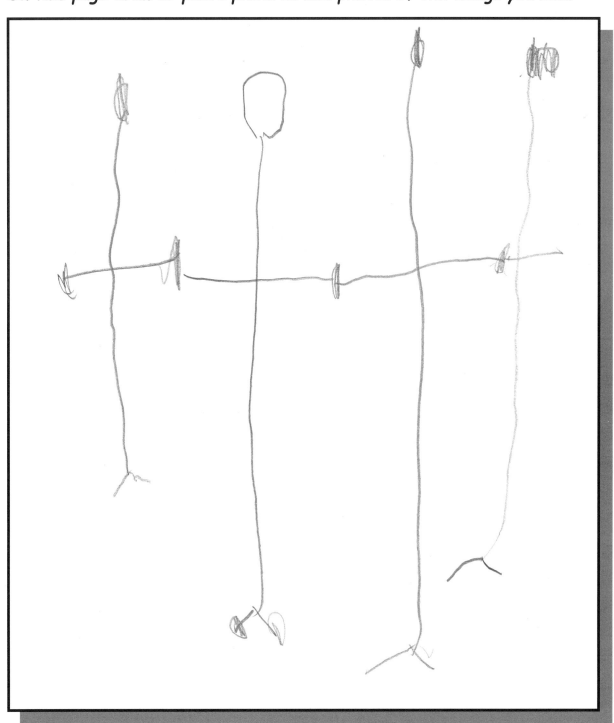

Page # _____   **My Travel Diary**

Today is [   ]   _The date is_ [   ]

A short list of TODAY'S special adventures

Someone I met: _____

Something special I saw: _____

Something new I learned: _____

Something I want to tell my friends about: _____
_____

Everything about TODAY: _____

_____

_____

_____

_____

_____

_____

_____

_____

_____

_____

_____

My Travel Diary

PICTURE PAGE

On this page draw or paste pictures and photos of the things you saw.

Page # _____

Today is [_____]   *The date is* [_____]

A short list of TODAY'S special adventures

Someone I met: _____

Something special I saw: _____

Something new I learned: _____

Something I want to tell my friends about: _____

_____

Everything about TODAY: _____

_____

_____

_____

_____

_____

_____

_____

_____

_____

_____

_____

My Travel Diary

PICTURE PAGE

On this page draw or paste pictures and photos of the things you saw.

VACATION SCORECARD

Packing

○ I packed much too much
○ I packed a little too much
○ I packed just the right amount
○ I packed a little too little
○ I packed much too little

Travel

○ I would have liked to have stayed much closer to home
○ I would have liked to have stayed a little closer to home
○ We traveled just the right distance
○ I would have liked to have gone a little farther from home
○ I would have liked to have gone much farther from home

Weather

○ The weather was much too hot
○ The weather was a little too warm
○ The weather was just right
○ The weather was a little too cool
○ The weather was much too cold

Activity

○ There was much too much to do
○ There was a little too much to do
○ There was just the right amount to do
○ There was not enough to do
○ There was nothing to do

Overall Rating

○ Perfect! The best vacation ever
○ Excellent. The trip was very nice
○ Very good. Fun, but could be better
○ OK. Not as fun as I had hoped.
○ Terrible! We should have stayed home

○ I would like to go again
○ I would not like to go again

Things I would do differently next time

_____
_____
_____
_____
_____
_____

Getting Ready

Oh no!!! It's time to go home. Your vacation fun is just about over!! But don't moan and groan! It's not the end of the world. If you lose your cool you may never go on a vacation again. Have a good return trip, and you'll be ready to jump right back into the swing of things as soon as you get home. There's still fun to be had, and plenty to tell your friends about your trip.

Time to pack again. Sometimes it's harder to pack for the trip home than it was to pack to go away, especially if you bought lots of souvenirs. Be careful not to forget anything! It's hard to get something back that you leave behind. Separate your clean and dirty clothes. If your swimsuit is wet, put it into a plastic bag.

Pack the things you'll want to use on the return trip in a travel bag or backpack you'll keep with you. Keep stuff like your games, pad and pencil, and this book in it. You might want postcards handy so you can write some on the way.

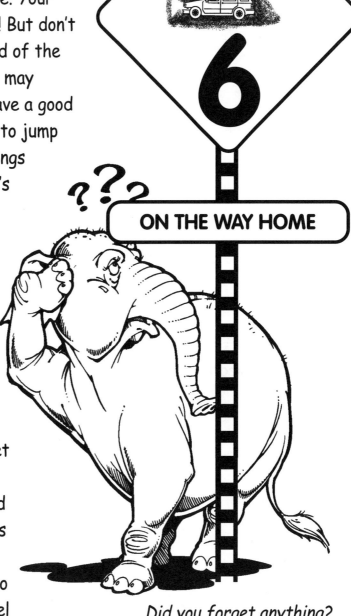

CHAPTER 6

ON THE WAY HOME

Did you forget anything?

The Return Trip

You can play all of the travel games that you played on the way. See if you're better at the games on the return trip because of the practice you had going. If you played spotting games, you might still have the lists on a pad, and you can pick up where you stopped and see if you can spot items you missed on the way.

You can play a "test your memory" game with your fellow travellers. Make up questions about the places you went, things you did, the most fun you had. What do you remember most about the trip? You'll be surprised at each person's different ideas. You'll wonder if you all went on the same trip!

Postcards and Letters

If you had such a good time on your trip that you forgot to send letters and postcards you had marked on your planning calendar, don't feel bad. You can take them with you and give them to your friends and relatives when you see them, or you can write messages on the way home. If you stop on the way, you might mail them, but <u>you</u> could get home before the postcards are delivered! Sometimes it's nice to pick up a few extras to keep or to show people you meet who are interested in the place you've been.

If you made new friends on your trip, be sure you have their addresses and phone numbers. Some day you can send them a note. If you stayed with friends or relatives, it's proper to send them a thank-you note!

Souvenirs and Keepsakes

It's always nice to have some souvenirs. Find a little something to remember the trip by before you leave. Pick something that will remind you of the fun you had and the things you did. There are many different things that you can get, but you must remember that you have to get them home, so think carefully before you pick up a souvenir you can't get home.

A T-shirt or poster with an armadillo on it would be a great souvenir from Texas, but a real, live armadillo would be a problem!

Souvenir Ideas

T-shirts, caps and patches are fun, and they're useful too! When you wear them people will ask you about your trip. Pennants and posters you can frame and hang in your room are good too. Mugs and cups, or desk items like pens, pads and paperweights are nice keepsakes if they have the name of the place and a picture on them. Try to pick things out that you can't get at home or that remind you of something special about the place you have been. Pennants and posters will last a long time. A T-shirt might not last forever, but it's more useful. Think carefully when you're in a souvenir shop, and don't buy just any item.

If you went to San Diego, California, and you wanted to remember your trip, the Lion T-shirt from the zoo would be one good choice, but the surfboard from the shop at the beach might not fit in your car or on the plane!

If you went to Cooperstown, New York, a Baseball Hall of Fame bat or jersey would be nice, but the life-size statue of Babe Ruth would be too hard to get home. (They wouldn't let you take it anyway, but you get the idea!)

Keepsakes — Your Own Travel Diary

The best keepsake you could have is the travel diary you kept in this book.

You can read everything you wrote, and refresh your memory about the things you did each day. You can add to it, color in your drawings, correct your spelling, or mark the things you did that you liked best. You can add photographs when your film is developed.

When you are home and your vacation trip is over, you can cut out the diary and picture pages and make your own book about your summer vacation.

Design a cover with a title and a picture on it. Slip on a plastic binder . . . Awesome, Dude, you wrote a book! It was fun! Show it to your friends and classmates. They'll see all the things you did and what a great time you had.

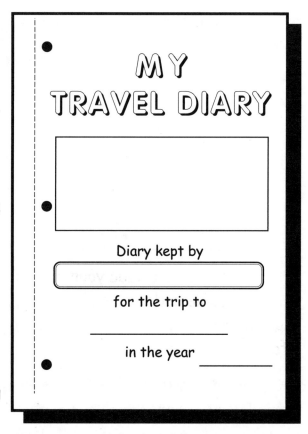

Make notes about things you brought with you that you didn't need, and things you wished you had brought but didn't.

Last but not least, be sure to thank whoever arranged your trip for taking you on a totally awesome vacation.

FREE INFORMATION IF YOU ASK

C H A P T E R 7

In the United States, there is a **tourist information office** in each state, and one in the District of Columbia, where the capital is.

A tourism office will be open 9:00 AM to 5:00 PM Monday to Friday. It may be in a different time zone. <u>Check the time zone map on Page 7!</u>

Remember to call or write as far in advance of your trip as you can. It may take six weeks for the material to reach you.

● If you **telephone**, have ready the name of the place you are going, the city and state it is in, and the address where you want the information mailed. The telephone call will be free only if the number is an "800" number. All other long-distance calls will cost money.

● If you **write** to a tourism office, be sure to include your name and home address so they know where to send the information you want. Be specific and give the names and addresses of the places you want information about.

WHERE TO WRITE

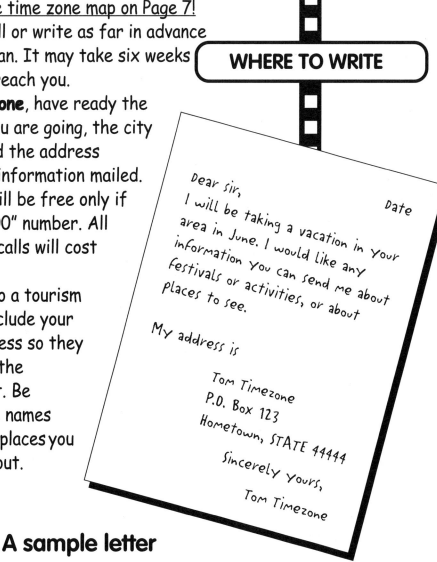

Dear Sir,

Date

I will be taking a vacation in your area in June. I would like any information you can send me about festivals or activities, or about places to see.

My address is

Tom Timezone
P.O. Box 123
Hometown, STATE 44444

Sincerely Yours,

Tom Timezone

A sample letter

═══ U.S. State Tourism Offices ═══

ALABAMA Bureau of Tourism
401 Adams Ave. Suite 126
Montgomery, AL 36103
☎ 1-800-ALABAMA
www.touralabama.org

ALASKA Travel Industry Assoc.
2600 Cordova Street
Suite 201
Anchorage, AK 99503
☎ 1-907-929-2200
www.travelalaska.com

ARIZONA Office of Tourism
2702 North 3rd St., Suite 4015
Phoenix, AZ 85004
☎ 1-888-520-3433
www.arizonaguide.com

ARKANSAS Division of Tourism
No. 1 Capitol Mall
Little Rock, AR 72201
☎ 1-800-643-8383
www.arkansas.com

CALIFORNIA Office of Tourism
PO Box 1499
Dept. TIA
Sacramento, CA 95812
☎ 1-800-862-2543
www.gocalif.com

COLORADO Travel and Tourism
Authority
1625 Broadway
Denver, CO 80202
☎ 1-800-Colorado
www.colorado.com

CONNECTICUT Office of Tourism
505 Hudson St.
Hartford, CT 06106
☎ 1-800-CT-BOUND
www.ctbound.org

DELAWARE Tourism Office
99 Kings Highway
Dover, DE 19901
☎ 1-800-441-8846
www.visitdelaware.net

DISTRICT OF COLUMBIA
(Washington DC area)
DC Committee to Promote
1212 New York Ave. NW, Suite 200
Washington, DC 20005
☎ 1-800-422-8644
www.washington.org

FLORIDA Division of Tourism
661 E. Jefferson St.
Tallahassee, FL 32301
☎ 1-888-7-FLA-USA
www.flausa.com

GEORGIA Dept. of Trade & Tourism
285 Peachtree Center Avenue NE
Suite 1000 and 1100
Atlanta, GA 30303
☎ 1-800-VISIT GA
www.georgia.org

HAWAII Visitor's Bureau
2270 Kalakaua Ave., Suite 801
Honolulu, HI 96815
☎ 1-800-Go Hawaii
www.gohawaii.com

IDAHO Travel Council
PO Box 83720
700 West State Street
Boise, ID 83720-0093
☎ 1-800-635-7820
www.visitid.org

ILLINOIS Bureau of Tourism
100 W. Randolf St., Suite 3-400
Chicago, IL 60610
☎ 1-312-814-4732
   1-800-2-CONNECT
www.enjoyillinois.com

INDIANA Tourism Division
Department of Commerce
One North Capitol, Suite 700
Indianapolis, IN 46204
☎ 1-800-289-6646
www.enjoyindiana.com

IOWA Department of Economic
Development, Division of Tourism
200 E. Grand Avenue
Des Moines, IA 50309
☎ 1-888-472-6035
www.traveliowa.com

KANSAS Dept. of Economic Dev., Div,
of Tourism
700 Southwest Harrison, Suite 1300
Topeka, KS 66603-3712
☎ 1-800-252-6727
www.kansas-travel.com

KENTUCKY Dept. of Travel development
Capitol Plaza Tower, 22nd floor
500 Mero St.
Frankfort, KY 40601
☎ 1-800-225-8747
www.kentuckytourism.com

LOUISIANA Office of Tourism
P.O. Box 94291
Baton Rouge, LA 70804
☎ 1-800-261-9144
www.louisianatravel.com

MAINE State Dev. Office
59 State House Station
Office of Tourism
Augusta, ME 04330
☎ 1-800 533-9595
www.visitmaine.com

MARYLAND Office of Tourism
217 East Redwood, 9th Floor
Baltimore, MD 21202
☎ 1-800-543-1036
www.mdisfun.org

MASSACHUSETTS Office of Tourism
10 Park Plaza, Suite 4510
Boston, MA 02116
☎ 1-800-227-6277
   1-800-SEE-BOSTON
www.massvacation.com

MICHIGAN Travel Bureau
201 North Washington Square
Lansing, MI 48913
☎ 1-800-5432-YES
www.michigan.org

MINNESOTA Office of Tourism
500 Metro Square
121 7th Place East
St. Paul, MN 55101
☎ 1-800-657-3700
www.exploreminnesota.com

MISSISSIPPI Division of Tourism
P.O. Box 1705
Ocean Springs, MS 39566-1705
☎ 1-800-WARMEST
www.visitmississippi.org

MISSOURI Division of Tourism
P.O. Box 1055
Truman State Office Building
Jefferson City, MO 65102
☎ 1-800-877-1234
www.missouritourism.org

MONTANA Travel Promotion
1424 9th Avenue
Helena, MT 59620
☎ 1-800-541-1447
www.visitmt.com

U.S. State Tourism Offices

NEBRASKA Division of Travel
P.O. Box 98913
Lincoln, NE 68509
☎ 1-800-228-4307
www.visitnebraska.org

NEVADA Commission of Tourism
401 North Carson Street
Carson City, NV 89701
☎ 1-800-NEVADA-8
www.travelnevada.com/

NEW HAMPSHIRE Office of Tourism
P.O. Box 1856
Concord, NH 03302-1856
☎ 1-603-271-2666
☎ 1-800-FUN-IN-NH
www.visitnh.gov

NEW JERSEY Division of Travel
P.O. Box 820
Trenton, NJ 08625
☎ 1-800-VISITNJ
www.visitnj.org

NEW MEXICO Tourism Department
491 Old Santa Fe Trail
Santa Fe, NM 87501
☎ 1-800-545-2040
www.newmexico.org

NEW YORK Division of Tourism
PO Box 2603
Albany, NY 12220-0603
☎ 1-800-CALL-NYS
www.iloveny.com

NORTH CAROLINA Travel & Tourism
Division
301 No. Wilmington St.
4324 Mail Service Center
Raleigh, NC 27626-2825
☎ 1-800-847-4862
www.visitnc.com

NORTH DAKOTA Tourism Department
Liberty Memorial Building
604 East Boulevard Avenue
Bismarck, ND 58505-0825
☎ 1-800-HELLO-ND
www.ndtourism.com

OHIO Office of Travel and Tourism
77 South High
P.O. Box 1001
Columbus, OH 43266
☎ 1-800-BUCKEYE
www.ohiotourism.com

OKLAHOMA Department of Tourism
P.O. Box 52002
Oklahoma City, OK 73152
☎ 1-800-652-6552
www.travelok.com
www.touroklahoma.com

OREGON Dept. of Tourism
P.O.Box 14070
Portland, OR 97293-0073
☎ 1-800-547-7842
www.traveloregon.com

PENNSYLVANIA Bureau of Travel
404 Forum Building
Harrisburg, PA 17120
☎ 1-800-237-4363
www.experiencepa.com

RHODE ISLAND Tourism Division
1 West Exchange Street
Providence, RI 02903
☎ 1-800-556-2484
www.visitrhodeisland.com

SOUTH CAROLINA Dept. of Parks,
Recreation & Tourism
1205 Pendleton Street, Suite 106
Columbia, SC 29201
☎ 1-803-734-1700
☎ 1-888-SC-SMILE
www.travelsc.com

SOUTH DAKOTA Division of Tourism
711 East Wells Ave.
Pierre, SD 57501-3369
☎ 1-800-S-DAKOTA
www.travelsd.com

TENNESSEE Tourist Development
P.O. Box 23170
Nashville, TN 37202
☎ 1-615-741-2158
☎ 1-800-GO-2-TENN
www.state.tn.us/tourdev

TEXAS Tourism Div. of Commerce
P.O. Box 12728 Capitol Station
Austin, TX 78711
☎ 1-800-888-8TEX
www.traveltex.com

UTAH Travel Council
Capitol Hill, Council Hall
Salt Lake City, UT 84114
☎ 1-801-538-1030
☎ 1-800-200-1160
www.utah.com

VERMONT Travel Division
134 State Street
Montpelier, VT 05602
☎ 1-800-VERMONT
www.1-800-Vermont.com

VIRGINIA Division of Tourism
901 East Byrd St.
Richmond, VA 23219
☎ 1-804-786-4484
☎ 1-800-VISIT-VA
www.virginia.org

WASHINGTON D.C. see **District of Columbia**

WASHINGTON State Dept. of Trade
& Tourism
520 Pike Street
Suite 1300
Seattle, WA 98101
☎ 1-206-461-5840
☎ 1-800-544-1800
www.seeseattle.org
www.tourismwa.gov/

WEST VIRGINIA Div. of Commerce
2101 Washington Street East
Charleston, WV 25305
☎ 1-800-225-5982
www.callwva.com

WISCONSIN Division of Tourism
201 West Washington Ave.
P.O. Box 7976
Madison, WI 53707
☎ 1-800-ESCAPES
www.travelwisconsin.com

WYOMING Travel Commission
Frank Norris J.Travel Center
Interstate 25 at College Drive
Cheyenne, WY 82002
☎ 1-800-225-5996
www.wyomingtourism.org

If you're interested ...

There is a small Island called **American Samoa** on the other side of the world that is governed by the United States, though it is not a state. Write to them and ask them to send information about their island.

AMERICAN SAMOA Tourism Office
Convention Center
PO Box 1147
Pago Pago, AS 96799
☎ 011-(684)-633-1092
www.samoanet.com/americansamoa

Canadian Provinces Tourism Offices

Each of Canada's provinces has an office you can call or write for information. Remember that it costs more to mail a letter to Canada than to another state. Ask your postmaster about the correct postage.

ALBERTA Travel
17811-116 Avenue
Edmonton, AB T5S2J2 Canada
☎ 1-800-661-8888
www.travelalberta.com

BRITISH COLUMBIA Tourism
P.O.Box 9830
Stn. Prov. Govt
Victoria, BC V8W9W5 Canada
☎ 1-800-hellobc
www.hellobc.com

MANITOBA Dept. of Cultural
Heritage & Tourism Travel
7th Floor, 155 Carlton St.
Winnepeg, MB R3C 3H8 Canada
☎ 1- 204- 945-3796
1-800-665-0040
www.travelmanitoba.com

NEW BRUNSWICK Sector Dev.
Officer (Tourism)
P.O. Box 6000
Clarkston, WA E3B 5G1 Canada
☎ 1-506-453-3009
1-800-561-0123
www.tourismnbcanada.com

NEWFOUNDLAND Industry Canada
P.O. Box 8950
John CabotBuilding-10 Barters Hill
St. Johns, Newfoundland,
NF A1B 3R9 Canada
☎ 1-709-772-4782
1-800-563-6353
www.gov.nf.ca/tourism

NORTHWEST TERRITORIES
ArcticTourism
P.O. Box 610
Yellowknife, NT XIA 2N5
Canada
☎ 1-867-873-7200
1-800-661-0788
www.nwttravel.nt.ca

NOVA SCOTIA Tourism Office
PO. Box 940 Station M
1505 Barrington St, 16th Floor
Halifax, NS B3J 2V9 Canada
☎ 1-902-426-3458
1-800-565-0000
www.explorens.com

ONTARIO Tourism
1 Concord Gate, 9th Floor
Toronto, ONT M3C3N6 Canada
☎ 1-800-ONTARIO
www.ontariotravel.net

PRINCE EDWARD ISLAND Tourism
P.O. Box 940
Charlottetown, PEI C1A 7M5
Canada
☎ 1-888-PEI-Play
www.peiplay.com

QUEBEC Office of Tourism
835 Avenue Wilfird-Laurier
Quebec, QC GIR2L3
Canada
☎ 1-877-BONJOUR
www.bonjourquebec.com

SASKATCHEWAN Director of
Tourism
1922 Park Street
Regina, SK S4P3V7
Canada
☎ 1-306-787-9124
1-877-2-ESCAPE
www.sasktourism.com

VANCOUVER
Plaza Level
200 Burrand Street
Clarkston, WA V6C3L6
Canada
☎ 1-604-683-2000
www.tourism-vancouver.org

YUKON Director of Tourism
PO Box 2703
Whitehorse, YT Y1A 2C6
Canada
☎ 1-867-667-5340
www.touryukon.com

Mexican Tourism Office

There is one toll-free number you can call from anywhere in the United States for information about vacations in Mexico. Call **1-800-446-3942** or you can contact the Mexican regional tourism office listed here. Also included is their website.

MEXICAN Tourism Office
Romulo O'Farril #262
Colonia Olivar De Lof Padres
Mexico City, DF 01780
Mexico
www.mexico-travel.com